TO

_____

from

_____

Real Questions...
Real Anwsers...

her
devotional

2
MINUTES A DAY
FOR TEENS

her
devotional

2

MINUTES A DAY

FOR TOONS

The quoted ideas expressed in this book (but not scripture verses) are not, in all cases, exact quotations, as some have been edited for clarity and brevity. In all cases, the author has attempted to maintain the speaker's original intent. In some cases, quoted material for this book was obtained from secondary sources, primarily print media. While every effort was made to ensure the accuracy of these sources, the accuracy cannot be guaranteed. For additions, deletions, corrections or clarifications in future editions of this text, please write FAMILY CHRISTIAN PRESS.

Scripture quotations are taken from:

The Holy Bible, New King James Version (NKJV) Copyright © 1982 by Thomas Nelson, Inc. Used by permission.

Holy Bible, New Living Translation, (NLT) Copyright © 1996. Used by permission of Tyndale House Publishers, Inc., Wheaton, Illinois 60189. All rights reserved.

New Century Version®. (NCV) Copyright © 1987, 1988, 1991 by Word Publishing, a division of Thomas Nelson, Inc. All rights reserved. Used by permission.

The Message (MSG) This edition issued by contractual arrangement with NavPress, a division of The Navigators, U.S.A. Originally published by NavPress in English as THE MESSAGE: The Bible in Contemporary Language copyright 2002-2003 by Eugene Peterson. All rights reserved.

The Holman Christian Standard Bible™ (HCSB) Copyright © 1999, 2000, 2001 by Holman Bible Publishers. Used by permission.

Cover Design by Kim Russell / Wahoo Designs
Page Layout by Bart Dawson

ISBN 1-58334-192-7
ISBN 978-158334-192-6
Printed in the United States of America

Table of Contents

her devotions

INTRODUCTION

You're Busy, But Not That Busy

Can you spare two minutes each day for God? Of course you can . . . and of course you should! No matter how busy you are, you should *never* allow the temptations and distractions of everyday living to distance you from your Creator.

Being a young woman in today's world isn't easy. This world offers limitless opportunities to stray from the path that God intends for your life. You are confronted with temptations and distractions that were unknown to previous generations. And, the world is changing so rapidly that, at times, it seems difficult to catch your breath and keep your balance. This little book is intended to help.

2 MINUTES A DAY

This book contains 31 short devotional readings of particular interest to young women like you. Each chapter contains a Bible verse, a brief devotional reading, quotations from noted Christian women (plus quotes from a few guys), and a prayer.

Do you have questions that you can't answer? Are you seeking to change some aspect of your life? Do you desire the eternal abundance and peace that can be yours through Christ? If so, ask for God's help and ask for it many times each day; starting with a regular, heartfelt morning devotional. Even two minutes is enough time to change your day . . . *and* your life.

INTRODUCTION

2 Minutes
a Day . . .
at a
Minimum

Be still, and know that I am God.

Psalm 46:10 NKJV

her devotional

As you organize your day and your life, where does God fit in? Do you "squeeze Him in" on Sundays and at mealtimes? Or do you consult Him more often than that?

This book asks that you give your undivided attention to God for *at least* two minutes each day. And make no mistake about it: The emphasis in the previous sentence should be placed on the words "at least." In truth, you should give God lots more time than a couple of minutes a day, but hey, it's a start!

Even if you're the busiest girl on the planet, you can still carve out a little time for God. And when you think about it, isn't that the very least you should do?

15

Think About It

God is more concerned with
the direction of your life
than with its speed.
Marie T. Freeman

The manifold rewards of a serious,
consistent prayer life demonstrate clearly
that time with our Lord should be
our first priority.
Shirley Dobson

Let's face it. None of us can do
a thousand things to the glory of God.
And, in our own vain attempt to do so,
we stand the risk of forfeiting
a precious thing.
Beth Moore

2 MINUTES A DAY ... AT A MINIMUM

A Timely Tip

Make God a Priority: Your days are probably filled to the brim with lots of obligations. But remember: No obligation is greater than the debt you owe to your Creator. So, make sure that you give Him the time He deserves, not only on Sundays, but also on every other day of the week.

A Prayer to the Father

Lord, let Your priorities be my priorities. Let Your Word be my guide. And let me spend time with You today, and let me grow in faith and in wisdom this day and every day. —Amen

2 MINUTES A DAY

Looking for God's Plan

The LORD says, "I will guide you along
the best pathway for your life.
I will advise you and watch over you."
Psalm 32:8 NLT

"What on earth does God intend for me to do with my life?" It's an easy question to ask, but for many of us, a difficult question to answer. Why? Because God's purposes aren't always clear to us. Sometimes we wander aimlessly in a wilderness of our own making. And sometimes, we struggle mightily against God in an unsuccessful attempt to find success and happiness through our own means, not His.

Are you genuinely trying to figure out God's purpose for your life? If so, you can be sure that with God's help, you *will* eventually discover it. So keep praying, and keep watching. And rest assured: God's got big plans for you . . . *very* big plans.

Think About It

God wants us to serve Him
with a willing spirit,
one that would choose no other way.

Beth Moore

With God, it's never "Plan B" or
"second best." It's always "Plan A."
And, if we let Him, He'll make something
beautiful of our lives.

Gloria Gaither

There is something incredibly comforting
about knowing that the Creator
is in control of your life.

Lisa Whelchel

LOOKING FOR . . . GOD'S PLAN

A Timely Tip

✿✿✿✿✿✿✿✿✿✿✿✿✿✿✿✿✿✿✿✿✿✿✿✿✿✿✿✿✿✿✿

Don't Be in Such a Hurry: Perhaps you're in a big hurry to understand God's unfolding plan for your life. If so, remember that God operates according to a perfect timetable. That timetable is His, not yours, so be patient. God has big things in store for you, but He may have quite a few lessons to teach you *before* you are fully prepared to do His will and fulfill His purpose.

✿✿✿✿✿✿✿✿✿✿✿✿✿✿✿✿✿✿✿✿✿✿✿✿✿✿✿✿✿✿✿

A Prayer to the Father

✿✿✿✿✿✿✿✿✿✿✿✿✿✿✿✿✿✿✿✿✿✿✿✿✿✿✿✿✿✿✿

Lord, You've got something you want me to do—help me to figure out exactly what it is. Give me Your blessings and lead me along a path that is pleasing to You . . . today, tomorrow, and forever. —Amen

✿✿✿✿✿✿✿✿✿✿✿✿✿✿✿✿✿✿✿✿✿✿✿✿✿✿✿✿✿✿✿

2 MINUTES A DAY

Perfectionism 101

Those who wait for perfect weather
will never plant seeds; those who look at
every cloud will never harvest crops.
Plant early in the morning, and work
until evening, because you don't know
if this or that will succeed.
They might both do well.

Ecclesiastes 11:4, 6 NCV

If you have become discouraged with your inability to be perfect, it's officially time to lighten up. Remember that when you accepted Christ as your Savior, God accepted you for all eternity. Now, it's *your* turn to accept yourself. When you do, you'll feel a tremendous weight being lifted from your shoulders. After all, pleasing God is simply a matter of obeying His commandments and accepting His Son. But as for pleasing everybody else: That's impossible!

Think About It

God is so inconceivably good.
He's not looking for perfection.
He already saw it in Christ.
He's looking for affection.
Beth Moore

What makes a Christian a Christian
is not perfection but forgiveness.
Max Lucado

Get ready for God to show you not only
His pleasure, but His approval.
Joni Eareckson Tada

God is bigger than your problems.
Whatever worries press upon you today,
put them in God's hands
and leave them there.
Billy Graham

PERFECTIONISM 101

Q: If God thinks I'm beautiful, why do I feel so below average?

A: Because you're trying to live up to impossible standards! If you listen to the messages that spew out of the media, you'll convince yourself that you can never be pretty enough, thin enough, smart enough, or rich enough. But God doesn't care about stuff like that, and neither should you. God loves you just like you are . . . and now, it's your turn to do the same thing.

A Prayer to the Father

Lord, I'm certainly not perfect, but you love me just as I am. Thank You for Your love and for Your Son. And, help me to become the person that You want me to become. —Amen

2 MINUTES A DAY

Tell Me, God: Why Do Bad Things Happen?

Can you understand the secrets of God? His limits are higher than the heavens; you cannot reach them! They are deeper than the grave; you cannot understand them! His limits are longer than the earth and wider than the sea.

Job 11:7-9 NCV

If God is good, and if He made the world, why do bad things happen? Part of that question is easy to answer, and part of it isn't. Let's get to the easy part first: Sometimes, bad things happen because people choose to disobey God's rules.

When people break the rules—especially God's rules—they make trouble for themselves *and* for others; it's unfortunate but it happens. But, on other occasions, bad things happen, and it's nobody's fault. So who is to blame then? Sometimes, nobody is to blame. Things just happen and we simply cannot know why. Thankfully, all our questions will be answered . . . some day.

The good news is this: The Bible promises that when we finally get to heaven, we will understand all the reasons behind God's plans. But until then, we must simply trust Him, knowing that, in the end, He will make things right.

2 MINUTES A DAY

Think About It

Every misfortune, every failure,
every loss may be transformed.
God has the power to transform
all misfortunes into "God-sends."
Mrs. Charles E. Cowman

Often the trials we mourn are really
gateways into the good things we long for.
Hannah Whitall Smith

Among the most joyful people I have
known have been some who seem to
have had no human reason for joy.
The sweet fragrance of Christ
has shown through their lives.
Elisabeth Elliot

WHY DO BAD THINGS HAPPEN?

And One More Thing . . .

⬇ ⬇ ⬇

Let's thank God for allowing us
to experience troubles
that drive us closer to Him.

Shirley Dobson

A Prayer to the Father

✿✿✿✿✿✿✿✿✿✿✿✿✿✿✿✿✿✿✿✿✿✿✿✿✿✿✿✿✿✿

Lord, sometimes I just don't understand why things turn out like they do. But even when I can't understand why bad things happen, I still know Who's in charge: You. And until that wonderful day when I understand everything, I will trust You. —Amen

✿✿✿✿✿✿✿✿✿✿✿✿✿✿✿✿✿✿✿✿✿✿✿✿✿✿✿✿✿✿

2 MINUTES A DAY

Praying for Friends . . . and Enemies

You have heard that it was said,
"Love your neighbor and hate
your enemies." But I say to you,
love your enemies.
Pray for those who hurt you.

Matthew 5:43, 44 NCV

It's usually pretty easy to pray for your friends and family members—all you have to do is find the time. But when it comes to praying for people who have hurt you, well that's a different matter entirely!

Like it or not, God says that you've got to pray for the folks you like *and* for the folks you don't like. Why? Well, maybe it's because God knows that He has already forgiven *you,* and now He thinks it's about time for you to forgive *them.*

Think About It

Prayer moves the arm that moves
the world.
Annie Armstrong

The things that we feel most deeply
we ought to learn to be silent about,
at least until we have talked them over
thoroughly with God.
Elisabeth Elliot

If you can't seem to forgive someone,
pray for that person and keep praying
for him or her until, with God's help,
you've removed the poison of
bitterness from your heart.
Marie T. Freeman

PRAYING FOR FRIENDS . . .

Think About It

But when you are praying, first forgive
anyone you are holding a grudge against,
so that your Father in heaven
will forgive your sins, too.
Mark 11:25 NLT

A Prayer to the Father

✿✿✿✿✿✿✿✿✿✿✿✿✿✿✿✿✿✿✿✿✿✿✿✿✿✿✿✿✿✿✿✿✿

Lord, I will pray for the people who have
hurt me. I know that when I free myself
from needless bitterness, I will become a
better person, and that's precisely the kind
of person I intend to become. —Amen

✿✿✿✿✿✿✿✿✿✿✿✿✿✿✿✿✿✿✿✿✿✿✿✿✿✿✿✿✿✿✿✿✿

Choices, Choices, Choices

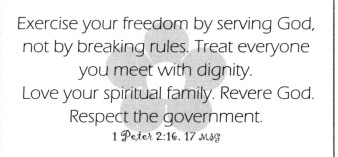

Exercise your freedom by serving God,
not by breaking rules. Treat everyone
you meet with dignity.
Love your spiritual family. Revere God.
Respect the government.
1 Peter 2:16, 17 MSG

Your life is a series of choices.

From the instant you wake up in the morning until the moment you nod off to sleep at night, you make lots of decisions: decisions about the things you do, decisions about the words you speak, and decisions about the thoughts you choose to think. Simply put, the quality of those decisions determines the quality of your life.

So, if you sincerely want to lead a life that is pleasing to God, you must make choices that are pleasing to Him. And you know what? He deserves no less . . . and neither, for that matter, do you.

Think About It

Faith is not a feeling;
it is action. It is a willed choice.
Elisabeth Elliot

There may be no trumpet sound or loud
applause when we make a right decision,
just a calm sense of resolution and peace.
Gloria Gaither

I do not know how the Spirit of Christ
performs it, but He brings us choices
through which we constantly change,
fresh and new, into His likeness.
Joni Eareckson Tada

CHOICES, CHOICES, CHOICES

Q: Is it true that I should pay close attention to my conscience?

A: You bet! That little voice inside your head will guide you down the right path *if* you listen carefully. Very often, your conscience will actually tell you what God wants you to do. So listen, learn, and behave accordingly.

A Prayer to the Father

Lord, You have given me a conscience that tells me right from wrong. Let me listen to that quiet voice so that I might do Your will and follow Your Word today and every day. —Amen

When
the Questions
Outnumber
the Answers

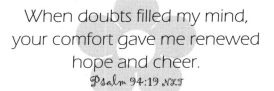

When doubts filled my mind,
your comfort gave me renewed
hope and cheer.
Psalm 94:19 NLT

So many questions and so few answers! If that statement seems to describe the current state of your spiritual life, don't panic. Even the most faithful Christians are overcome by occasional bouts of fear and doubt. You are no different.

When you feel that your faith is being tested to its limits, seek the comfort and assurance of the One who sent His Son as a sacrifice for you. And remember: Even when you feel very distant from God, God is never distant from you. When you sincerely seek His presence, He will touch your heart, calm your fears, and restore your soul.

Think About It

Ignoring Him by neglecting
prayer and Bible reading
will cause you to doubt.
Anne Graham Lotz

Mark it down. God never turns away
the honest seeker. Go to God with
your questions. You may not find all
the answers, but in finding God,
you know the One who does.
Max Lucado

We are most vulnerable to the piercing
winds of doubt when we distance
ourselves from the mission and fellowship
to which Christ has called us.
Joni Eareckson Tada

WHEN THE QUESTIONS OUTNUMBER . . .

A Timely Tip

✿✿✿✿✿✿✿✿✿✿✿✿✿✿✿✿✿✿✿✿✿✿✿✿✿✿✿✿✿✿✿✿✿✿

Got Questions? God has answers! If you're faced with too many questions and too few answers, slow down, and talk to your Father in heaven. When you do, you'll discover that He usually has many more answers than you have questions.

✿✿✿✿✿✿✿✿✿✿✿✿✿✿✿✿✿✿✿✿✿✿✿✿✿✿✿✿✿✿✿✿✿✿

A Prayer to the Father

✿✿✿✿✿✿✿✿✿✿✿✿✿✿✿✿✿✿✿✿✿✿✿✿✿✿✿✿✿✿✿✿✿✿

Lord, even when I have questions I can't answer, I will turn this day over to You. I know that with You in charge of my life, I will be directed and protected. Thank You, God, for leading me along the path that was first walked by Your Son. —Amen

✿✿✿✿✿✿✿✿✿✿✿✿✿✿✿✿✿✿✿✿✿✿✿✿✿✿✿✿✿✿✿✿✿✿

2 MINUTES A DAY

Setting the Right Example

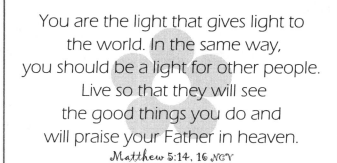

You are the light that gives light to
the world. In the same way,
you should be a light for other people.
Live so that they will see
the good things you do and
will praise your Father in heaven.
Matthew 5:14, 16 NCV

Like it or not, your behavior is a powerful example to others. The question is not *whether* you will be an example to your family and friends; the question is precisely *what kind* of example will you be?

Corrie ten Boom advised, "Don't worry about what you do not understand. Worry about what you do understand in the Bible but do not live by." And that's sound advice because your family and friends are always watching . . . and so, for that matter, is God.

Think About It

Your light is the truth of the Gospel
message itself as well as your witness
as to Who Jesus is and what
He has done for you. Don't hide it.

Anne Graham Lotz

Among the most joyful people I have
known have been some who seem to
have had no human reason for joy.
The sweet fragrance of Christ
has shown through their lives.

Elisabeth Elliot

More depends on my walk than my talk.

D. L. Moody

SETTING THE RIGHT EXAMPLE

Q: Why is it so much easier to talk about being a good person than it is to actually be one?

A: Face it: Talking about your beliefs is easy. But, making your actions match your words is much harder! Why? Because you are a normal human being, and that means that you can be tempted by stuff *and* by people. Nevertheless, if you *really* want to be honest with yourself, then you must make your actions match your beliefs.

A Prayer to the Father

✿✿✿✿✿✿✿✿✿✿✿✿✿✿✿✿✿✿✿✿✿✿✿✿✿✿✿✿✿✿✿✿

Lord, there is a right way and a wrong way to live. Let me live according to Your rules, not the world's rules. Your path is right for me, God; let me follow it every day of my life. —Amen

✿✿✿✿✿✿✿✿✿✿✿✿✿✿✿✿✿✿✿✿✿✿✿✿✿✿✿✿✿✿✿✿

2 MINUTES A DAY

I Want It, Lord, and I Want It Now!

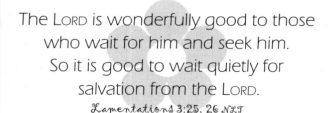

The LORD is wonderfully good to those
who wait for him and seek him.
So it is good to wait quietly for
salvation from the LORD.
Lamentations 3:25, 26 NLT

The dictionary defines the word *patience* as "the ability to be calm, tolerant, and understanding." If that describes you, you can skip the rest of this page. But, if you're like most of us, you'd better keep reading.

For most of us, patience is a hard thing to master. Why? Because we have lots of things we want, and we want them NOW (if not sooner). But the Bible tells us that we must learn to wait patiently for the things that God has in store for us.

The next time you find your patience tested to the limit, remember that the world unfolds according to God's timetable, not yours. Sometimes, you must wait patiently, and that's as it should be. After all, think how patient God has been with you!

2 MINUTES A DAY

Think About It

How do you wait upon the Lord?
First you must learn to sit at His feet
and take time to listen to His words.

Kay Arthur

Let me encourage you to continue to wait
with faith. God may not perform a miracle,
but He is trustworthy to touch you and
make you whole where there
used to be a hole.

Lisa Whelchel

God never gives up on you,
so don't you ever give up on Him.

Marie T. Freeman

I WANT IT, LORD, AND I WANT IT NOW!

A Timely Tip

✿✿✿✿✿✿✿✿✿✿✿✿✿✿✿✿✿✿✿✿✿✿✿✿✿✿✿✿✿✿✿✿✿✿✿✿

Take a deep breath, a very deep breath: If you think you're about to say or do something you'll regret later, slow down and take a deep breath, or two deep breaths, or ten, or . . . well you get the idea.

✿✿✿✿✿✿✿✿✿✿✿✿✿✿✿✿✿✿✿✿✿✿✿✿✿✿✿✿✿✿✿✿✿✿✿✿

A Prayer to the Father

✿✿✿✿✿✿✿✿✿✿✿✿✿✿✿✿✿✿✿✿✿✿✿✿✿✿✿✿✿✿✿✿✿✿✿✿

Lord, sometimes I can be a very impatient person. Slow me down and calm me down. Let me trust in Your plan, Father; let me trust in Your timetable; and let me trust in Your love for me. —Amen

✿✿✿✿✿✿✿✿✿✿✿✿✿✿✿✿✿✿✿✿✿✿✿✿✿✿✿✿✿✿✿✿✿✿✿✿

2 MINUTES A DAY

Are You Here, God . . . and Are You Listening?

Do not be afraid or discouraged.
For the LORD your God is with you
wherever you go.
Joshua 1:9 NLT

Do you ever wonder if God really hears your prayers? If so, you're in good company: lots of very faithful Christians have wondered the same thing. In fact, some of the biggest heroes in the Bible had their doubts—and so, perhaps, will you. But when you have your doubts, remember this: God isn't on vacation, and He hasn't moved out of town. God isn't taking a coffee break, and He isn't snoozing on the couch. He's right here, right now, listening to your thoughts and prayers, watching over your every move.

As the demands of everyday life weigh down upon you, you may be tempted to ignore God's presence or—worse yet—to rebel against His commandments. But, when you quiet yourself and acknowledge His presence, God touches your heart and restores your spirits. So why not let Him do it right now?

2 MINUTES A DAY

Think About It

Through the death and broken body
of Jesus Christ on the Cross,
you and I have been given access
to the presence of God when
we approach Him by faith in prayer.
Anne Graham Lotz

It is God to whom and with whom
we travel, and while He is the End
of our journey, He is also
at every stopping place.
Elisabeth Elliot

Life isn't life without some divine decisions
that our mortal minds simply
cannot comprehend.
Beth Moore

ARE YOU HERE, GOD . . .

Q: If God is everywhere, why does He sometimes seem so far away?

A: The answer to that question, of course, has nothing to do with God and everything to do with us. God sometimes seems far away because we have allowed ourselves to become distant from Him, not vice versa.

A Prayer to the Father

✿✿✿✿✿✿✿✿✿✿✿✿✿✿✿✿✿✿✿✿✿✿✿✿✿✿✿✿✿✿✿✿✿✿✿✿

Dear Lord, You are with me when I am strong and when I am weak. You never leave my side, even when it seems to me that You are far away. Today and every day, let me trust Your promises and let me feel Your love. —Amen

✿✿✿✿✿✿✿✿✿✿✿✿✿✿✿✿✿✿✿✿✿✿✿✿✿✿✿✿✿✿✿✿✿✿✿✿

When People Are Cruel

Do not fret because of evildoers;
don't envy the wicked.
Proverbs 24:19 NLT

Face

it: Sometimes people can be *very* cruel. And when people are unkind to you *or* to your friends, you may be tempted to strike back in anger. Don't do it! Instead, remember that God corrects other people's behaviors in His own way, and He doesn't need your help. And remember that God has commanded you to forgive others, just as you, too, must sometimes seek forgiveness from *them*.

So, when other people are cruel, as they most certainly will be from time to time, what should you do? 1. Politely speak up for yourself (*and* for people who can't speak up for *themselves*); 2. Forgive everybody as quickly as you can; 3. Leave the rest up to God; and 4. Get on with your life.

Think About It

Reject the road to cynicism.
Catherine Marshall

It is the duty of every Christian
to be Christ to his neighbor.
Martin Luther

Our pain is with us for a little while.
Our God is with us forever.
Marie T. Freeman

WHEN PEOPLE ARE CRUEL

And One More Thing . . .

↓   ↓   ↓

Just pray for a tough hide
and a tender heart.
Ruth Bell Graham

A Prayer to the Father

✿✿✿✿✿✿✿✿✿✿✿✿✿✿✿✿✿✿✿✿✿✿✿✿✿✿✿✿✿✿✿✿✿

Lord, just as You have forgiven me, I am going to forgive others. When I forgive others, I not only obey Your commandments, but I also free myself from bitterness and regret. Forgiveness is Your way, Lord, and I will make it my way, too. —Amen

✿✿✿✿✿✿✿✿✿✿✿✿✿✿✿✿✿✿✿✿✿✿✿✿✿✿✿✿✿✿✿✿✿

2 MINUTES A DAY

Searching for the Right Mr. Right

Now these three remain: faith, hope, and love. But the greatest of these is love.

1 Corinthians 13:13 HCSB

Oh, how glorious are the dreams of love—but oh, how tough it is to turn those dreams into reality! If you're still searching for Mr. Right (and if you're reading this book, you probably are), be patient, be prudent, and be picky. Look for a guy whose values you respect, whose behavior you approve of, and whose faith you admire. Remember that appearances can be deceiving *and* tempting, so watch your step. And when it comes to the important task of building a lifetime relationship with the guy of your dreams, pray about it! God is waiting to give His approval—or not—but He won't give it until He's asked. So ask, listen, and decide accordingly.

2 MINUTES A DAY

Think About It

Whatever you love most, be it sports,
pleasure, business or God,
that is your god.
Billy Graham

Since the Christian's Point of Reference is
the Bible, it's a happy couple
who look there for guidance.
Ruth Bell Graham

The love life of the Christian is
a crucial battleground.
There, if nowhere else, it will be
determined who is Lord: the world,
the self, and the devil—or the Lord Christ.
Elisabeth Elliot

SEARCHING FOR THE RIGHT MR. RIGHT

Q: How Far Is Too Far?

A: The Bible is right: Your body is, indeed, a temple. And if a guy won't keep his hands to himself, he's trying to trash that temple. Don't let him do it! And remember: It's not okay to trash the temple "just a little bit"—don't trash it *at all*.

A Prayer to the Father

✿✿✿✿✿✿✿✿✿✿✿✿✿✿✿✿✿✿✿✿✿✿✿✿✿✿✿✿✿✿✿✿✿✿✿

Lord, I will let You rule over every aspect of my life, including my relationships. And I know that when I do, You will help me make choices that are right for me, today and every day that I live. —Amen

✿✿✿✿✿✿✿✿✿✿✿✿✿✿✿✿✿✿✿✿✿✿✿✿✿✿✿✿✿✿✿✿✿✿✿

2 MINUTES A DAY

When Being a Christian Isn't Easy

For God has not given us a spirit of
fear and timidity, but of power, love,
and self-discipline. So you must never
be ashamed to tell others
about our Lord.

2 Timothy 1:7, 8 NLT

It's hard being a Christian some-times, especially when the world keeps pumping out messages that are contrary to your faith.

The media is working around the clock in an attempt to rearrange your priorities. The media says that your appearance, your clothes, your relationships with guys, and partying are "ALL-IMPORTANT". But guess what? Those messages are lies. The "all-important" things in your life have little to do with parties and appearances. The all-important things in life have to do with your faith, your family, and your future.

Are you willing to stand up for your faith? Are you willing to stand up and be counted, not just in church, where it's rela-tively easy to be a Christian, but also out there in the "real" world, where it's hard? Hopefully so, because you owe it to God *and* you owe it to yourself.

2 MINUTES A DAY

Think About It

Jesus draws near to those who
are suffering—especially when
the suffering is for His sake.
Anne Graham Lotz

Suffering is never for nothing.
It is that you and I might be conformed to
the image of Christ.
Elisabeth Elliot

I have discovered that when I please Christ,
I end up inadvertently serving others
far more effectively.
Beth Moore

WHEN BEING A CHRISTIAN ISN'T EASY

A Timely Tip

✿✿✿✿✿✿✿✿✿✿✿✿✿✿✿✿✿✿✿✿✿✿✿✿✿✿✿✿✿✿✿✿✿✿

Put Peer Pressure to Work For You:

Make up your mind to hang out with people who will put pressure on you to become a better person.

✿✿✿✿✿✿✿✿✿✿✿✿✿✿✿✿✿✿✿✿✿✿✿✿✿✿✿✿✿✿✿✿✿✿

A Prayer to the Father

✿✿✿✿✿✿✿✿✿✿✿✿✿✿✿✿✿✿✿✿✿✿✿✿✿✿✿✿✿✿✿✿✿✿

Lord, when it's difficult being a Christian, give me the courage and the wisdom to stand up for my faith. Christ made the ultimate sacrifice for me; let me now stand up for Him! —Amen

✿✿✿✿✿✿✿✿✿✿✿✿✿✿✿✿✿✿✿✿✿✿✿✿✿✿✿✿✿✿✿✿✿✿

Sharing My Faith Without Being "Preachy"

Be wise in the way you act
with people who are not believers,
making the most of every opportunity.
Colossians 4:5 NCV

How can I share my faith without sounding "holier than thou"?

Here are things to remember:

1. Be humble.

2. Be sincere.

3. Don't be so anxious to talk about your own beliefs that you forget to listen to the other person.

4. Remember that the life you lead (the way that you demonstrate your faith in action) is usually much more important that the words you speak. So don't just talk like a Christian; behave like one, too.

2 MINUTES A DAY

Think About It

One of the best ways to witness
to family, friends, and neighbors
is to let them see the difference Jesus
has made in your life.

Anne Graham Lotz

We must mirror God's love in the midst
of a world full of hatred. We are the mirrors
of God's love, so we may show
Jesus by our lives.

Corrie ten Boom

God has ordained that others may see
the reality of His presence by
the illumination our lives shed forth.

Beth Moore

SHARING MY FAITH . . .

Q: What if I'm uncomfortable talking about my faith?

A: Remember: you're not giving the State of the Union Address—you're having a conversation. And besides, if you're not sure what to say, a good place to start is by asking questions, not making speeches.

A Prayer to the Father

Lord, the life that I live and the words that I speak will tell the world how I feel about You. Today and every day, let my testimony be worthy of You. Let my words be sure and true, and let my actions point others to You. —Amen

2 MINUTES A DAY

Expectations, Expectations, Expectations

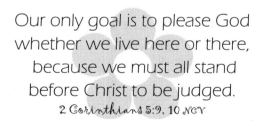

Our only goal is to please God
whether we live here or there,
because we must all stand
before Christ to be judged.
2 Corinthians 5:9, 10 NCV

As a young woman living in the 21st century, you know that demands can be high, and expectations even higher. The media delivers an endless stream of messages that tell you how to look, how to behave, how to eat, and how to dress. The media's expectations are impossible to meet—God's are not. God doesn't expect you to be perfect . . . and neither should you.

Remember: The expectations that *really* matter are God's expectations. Everything else takes a back seat. So do your best to please God, and don't worry too much about what other people think. And, when it comes to meeting the unrealistic expectations of a world gone nuts, forget about trying to be perfect—it's impossible.

2 MINUTES A DAY

Think About It

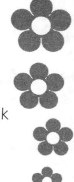

We get into trouble when we think
we *know* what to do and
we stop *asking God*
if we're doing it.

Stormie Omartian

Your will should be corrected to become
identified with God's will.
You must not bend God's will to suit yours.

St. Augustine

Yielding to the will of God is simply letting
His Holy Spirit have His way in our lives.

Shirley Dobson

EXPECTATIONS, EXPECTATIONS . . .

And One More Thing . . .

↓ ↓ ↓

You will get untold flak for prioritizing
God's revealed and present will for
your life over man's . . .
but, boy, is it worth it.

Beth Moore

A Prayer to the Father

✿✿✿✿✿✿✿✿✿✿✿✿✿✿✿✿✿✿✿✿✿✿✿✿✿✿✿✿✿✿✿

Lord, this world has so many expectations
of me, but today I will not seek to meet the
world's expectations; I will do my best to
meet Your expectations. I will make You my
ultimate priority, Lord, by serving You, by
praising You, by loving You, and by obeying
You. —Amen

✿✿✿✿✿✿✿✿✿✿✿✿✿✿✿✿✿✿✿✿✿✿✿✿✿✿✿✿✿✿✿

2 MINUTES A DAY

In Search of Encouraging Words

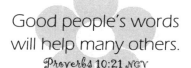

Good people's words
will help many others.
Proverbs 10:21 NCV

Life

is a team sport, and all of us need occasional pats on the back from our teammates. As Christians, we are called upon to spread the Good News of Christ, and we are also called to spread a message of encouragement and hope to the world.

Whether you realize it or not, many people with whom you come in contact every day are in desperate need of a smile or an encouraging word. The world can be a difficult place, and countless friends and family members may be troubled by the challenges of everyday life. Since you don't always know who needs your help, the best strategy is to try to encourage all the people who cross your path. So today, be a world-class source of encouragement to everyone you meet. Never has the need been greater.

Think About It

A single word,
if spoken in a friendly spirit,
may be sufficient to turn one
from dangerous error.
Fanny Crosby

Encouragement starts at home,
but it should never end there.
Marie T. Freeman

He climbs highest who helps another up.
Zig Ziglar

IN SEARCH OF ENCOURAGING WORDS

Think About It

You must warn each other every day,
as long as it is called "today,"
so that none of you will be deceived
by sin and hardened against God.
Hebrews 3:13 NLT

A Prayer to the Father

✿✿✿✿✿✿✿✿✿✿✿✿✿✿✿✿✿✿✿✿✿✿✿✿✿✿✿✿✿✿✿✿✿

Dear Lord, let me celebrate the accomplishments of others. Make me a source of genuine, lasting encouragement to my family and friends. And let my words and actions be worthy of Your Son, the One who has given me life abundant *and* life eternal. —Amen

✿✿✿✿✿✿✿✿✿✿✿✿✿✿✿✿✿✿✿✿✿✿✿✿✿✿✿✿✿✿✿✿✿

2 MINUTES A DAY

Mary and Martha

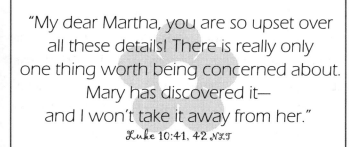

"My dear Martha, you are so upset over
all these details! There is really only
one thing worth being concerned about.
Mary has discovered it—
and I won't take it away from her."

Luke 10:41, 42 NLT

As Jesus and the disciples continued on their way to Jerusalem, they came to a village where a woman named Martha welcomed them into her home. Her sister, Mary, sat at the Lord's feet, listening to what he taught. But Martha was worrying over the big dinner she was preparing. She came to Jesus and said, "Lord, doesn't it seem unfair to you that my sister just sits here while I do all the work? Tell her to come and help me." But the Lord said to her, "My dear Martha, you are so upset over all these details! There is really only one thing worth being concerned about. Mary has discovered it—and I won't take it away from her."

Luke 10:38-42 NLT

Okay, after that rather long Bible passage, your two minute devotional is almost up, so we'll make it short and sweet: Martha was concerned with doing things *for* Jesus. Mary was concerned with being *with* Jesus. Mary made the better choice. Why? Because we need to be *with* Christ before we start do things *for* Him. End of lesson.

2 MINUTES A DAY

Think About It

Think of this—we may live together
with Him here and now,
a daily walking with Him who loved us
and gave Himself for us.
Elisabeth Elliot

Begin to know Him now, and finish never.
Oswald Chambers

Major on Jesus Christ. Make Him
the preeminent One in your life.
Warren Wiersbe

MARY AND MARTHA

And One More Thing . . .

⬇   ⬇   ⬇

Jesus is the personal approach from
the unseen God coming so near that
he becomes inescapable. You don't have
to find him—you just have
to consent to be found.

E. Stanley Jones

A Prayer to the Father

❀❀❀❀❀❀❀❀❀❀❀❀❀❀❀❀❀❀❀❀❀❀❀❀❀❀❀❀

Lord, You sent Jesus to save the world
and to save me. I will praise You for Your
Son, and I will follow Him, today and forever.
—Amen

❀❀❀❀❀❀❀❀❀❀❀❀❀❀❀❀❀❀❀❀❀❀❀❀❀❀❀❀

A Rule That's as Good as Gold

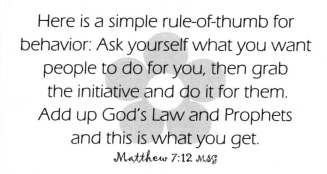

Here is a simple rule-of-thumb for
behavior: Ask yourself what you want
people to do for you, then grab
the initiative and do it for them.
Add up God's Law and Prophets
and this is what you get.
Matthew 7:12 MSG

Some rules are easier to understand than they are to live by. Jesus told us that we should treat other people in the same way that we want to be treated: that's the Golden Rule. But sometimes, especially when we're feeling pressure from friends, or when we're tired or upset, obeying the Golden Rule can seem like an impossible task—but it's not.

God wants us to treat other people with respect, kindness, and courtesy. He wants us to rise above our own imperfections, and He wants us to treat others with unselfishness and love. To make it short and sweet, God wants us to obey the Golden Rule, and He knows we can do it.

So if you're wondering how to treat someone else, ask the person you see every time you look into the mirror. The answer you receive will tell you exactly what to do.

2 MINUTES A DAY

Think About It

We should behave to our friends
as we would wish our friends
to behave to us.

Aristotle

The Golden Rule starts at home,
but it should never stop there.

Marie T. Freeman

What is your focus today?
Joy comes when it is Jesus first,
others second . . . then you.

Kay Arthur

A RULE THAT'S AS GOOD AS GOLD

And One More Thing . . .

↓   ↓   ↓

There are only two duties required of us—the love of God and the love of our neighbor, and the surest sign of discovering whether we observe these duties is the love of our neighbor.

St. Teresa of Avila

A Prayer to the Father

❀❀❀❀❀❀❀❀❀❀❀❀❀❀❀❀❀❀❀❀❀❀❀❀❀❀❀❀

Lord, in all aspects of my life, let me treat others as I wish to be treated. The Golden Rule is Your rule, Father; let me make it mine. —Amen

❀❀❀❀❀❀❀❀❀❀❀❀❀❀❀❀❀❀❀❀❀❀❀❀❀❀❀❀

2 MINUTES A DAY

Too Many Temptations

But remember that the temptations that come into your life are no different from what others experience. And God is faithful. He will keep the temptation from becoming so strong that you can't stand up against it. When you are tempted, he will show you a way out so that you will not give in to it.

1 Corinthians 10:13 NLT

How hard is it to bump into temptation in this crazy world? Not very hard. The devil, it seems, is working overtime these days, while causing pain and heartache in more places and in more ways than ever before. As Christians, we must remain strong. Not only must we resist Satan when he confronts us, but we must also avoid those places where Satan can most easily tempt us. As believing Christians, we must beware, and we must earnestly wrap ourselves in the protection of God's Holy Word. When we do, we are secure.

Think About It

Jesus faced every temptation known
to humanity so that
He could identify with us.
Beth Moore

The devil's most devilish when respectable.
Elizabeth Barrett Browning

In the worst temptations nothing can
help us but faith that God's Son has
put on flesh, sits at the right hand
of the Father, and prays for us.
There is no mightier comfort.
Martin Luther

TOO MANY TEMPTATIONS

A Timely Tip

✿✿✿✿✿✿✿✿✿✿✿✿✿✿✿✿✿✿✿✿✿✿✿✿✿✿✿✿✿

We Live in a "Temptation Nation"
At every turn in the road, or so it seems, somebody is trying to tempt you with something. Your job is to steer clear of temptation . . . and to *keep steering clear* as long as you live.

✿✿✿✿✿✿✿✿✿✿✿✿✿✿✿✿✿✿✿✿✿✿✿✿✿✿✿✿✿

A Prayer to the Father

✿✿✿✿✿✿✿✿✿✿✿✿✿✿✿✿✿✿✿✿✿✿✿✿✿✿✿✿✿

Lord, temptation is everywhere! Help me turn from it and to run from it! Let me keep Christ in my heart, and let me put the devil in his place: far away from me! —Amen

✿✿✿✿✿✿✿✿✿✿✿✿✿✿✿✿✿✿✿✿✿✿✿✿✿✿✿✿✿

2 MINUTES A DAY

Grace for Today . . . and Forever

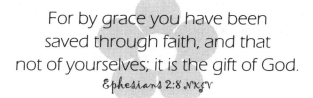

For by grace you have been
saved through faith, and that
not of yourselves; it is the gift of God.

Ephesians 2:8 NKJV

God's grace is not earned

. . . thank goodness! To earn God's love and His gift of eternal life would be far beyond the abilities of even the most righteous girl or guy. Thankfully, God's grace is not an earthly reward for righteous behavior; it is a spiritual gift that can be accepted by believers who dedicate themselves to God through Christ. When we accept Christ into our hearts, we are saved by His grace.

As you think about the day ahead, praise God for His blessings. He is the Giver of all things good. Praise Him today and forever.

2 MINUTES A DAY

Think About It

God does amazing works through
prayers that seek to extend
His grace to others.
Shirley Dobson

What grace calls you to do,
grace provides.
Grace is power.
Kay Arthur

God's grace and power seem to
reach their peak when
we are at our weakest point.
Anne Graham Lotz

GRACE FOR TODAY . . . AND FOREVER

Q: When should I start getting ready to die?

A: Face it: Death is a fact of life, and nobody knows when or where it's going to happen. So when it comes to making plans for life here on earth *and* for life eternal, you'd better be ready to live—*and* to die—right now.

A Prayer to the Father

✿✿✿✿✿✿✿✿✿✿✿✿✿✿✿✿✿✿✿✿✿✿✿✿✿✿✿✿✿✿✿✿

Lord, I'm only here on earth for a brief visit. Heaven is my real home. You've given me the gift of eternal life through Your Son Jesus. I accept Your gift, Lord. And I'll share Your Good News so that others, too, might come to know Christ's healing touch. —Amen

✿✿✿✿✿✿✿✿✿✿✿✿✿✿✿✿✿✿✿✿✿✿✿✿✿✿✿✿✿✿✿✿

2 MINUTES A DAY

Love
One Another

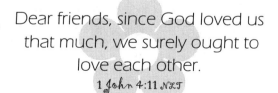

Dear friends, since God loved us
that much, we surely ought to
love each other.
1 John 4:11 NLT

Christ's words are clear: we are to love God first, and secondly, we are to love others as we love ourselves (Matthew 22:37-40). These two commands are seldom easy, and because we are imperfect people, we often fall short. But God's Word commands us to try and to *keep trying* as long as we live.

The Christian path is an exercise in love and forgiveness. If we are to walk in Christ's footsteps, we must forgive those who have done us harm, and we must accept Christ's love by sharing it freely with family, friends, neighbors, and the world.

Think About It

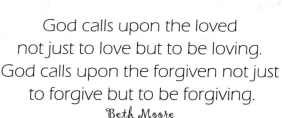

God calls upon the loved
not just to love but to be loving.
God calls upon the forgiven not just
to forgive but to be forgiving.

Beth Moore

Love is not soft as water is; it is solid
as a rock on which the waves of hatred
beat in vain.

Corrie ten Boom

Line by line, moment by moment,
special times are etched into our memories
in the permanent ink of everlasting love
in our relationships.

Gloria Gaither

LOVE ONE ANOTHER

And One More Thing . . .

⬇   ⬇   ⬇

When God measures a person,
He puts the tape around the heart
instead of the head.

Anonymous

A Prayer to the Father

✿✿✿✿✿✿✿✿✿✿✿✿✿✿✿✿✿✿✿✿✿✿✿✿✿✿✿✿✿✿✿✿✿✿✿✿

Lord, you have given me the gift of love and You've asked me to share it. The gift of love is a precious gift indeed. Let me nurture, love, and treasure it. And, help me remember that the essence of love is not to receive it, but to give it, today and forever. —Amen

✿✿✿✿✿✿✿✿✿✿✿✿✿✿✿✿✿✿✿✿✿✿✿✿✿✿✿✿✿✿✿✿✿✿✿✿

When My Prayers Go Unanswered

Trust in the LORD with all your heart;
do not depend on
your own understanding.

Proverbs 3:5 NLT

God answers our prayers.

What God does not do is this: He does not always answer our prayers as soon as we might like, and He does not always answer our prayers by saying "Yes." God isn't an order-taker, and He's not some sort of cosmic vending machine. Sometimes—even when we want something very badly—our loving Heavenly Father responds to our requests by saying "No", and we must accept His answer, even if we don't understand it.

God answers prayers not only according to *our* wishes but also according to *His* master plan. We cannot know that plan, but we can know the Planner . . . and we must trust His wisdom, His righteousness, and His love. Always.

2 MINUTES A DAY

Think About It

Faith is nothing more or less than
actively trusting God.
Catherine Marshall

If my life is surrendered to God, all is well.
Let me not grab it back, as though
it were in peril in His hand but
would be safer in mine!
Elisabeth Elliot

I must often be glad that certain
past prayers of my own
were not granted.
C. S. Lewis

WHEN MY PRAYERS GO UNANSWERED

A Timely Tip

✿✿✿✿✿✿✿✿✿✿✿✿✿✿✿✿✿✿✿✿✿✿✿✿✿✿

When God says "No," that's good!
Why? Because God *knows* what's best;
God *wants* what's best; and God is trying
to lead *you* to a place that is best for you. So
trust Him . . . especially when He says "No."

✿✿✿✿✿✿✿✿✿✿✿✿✿✿✿✿✿✿✿✿✿✿✿✿✿✿

A Prayer to the Father

✿✿✿✿✿✿✿✿✿✿✿✿✿✿✿✿✿✿✿✿✿✿✿✿✿✿

Dear Lord, I will be a woman of prayer.
I will take everything to You in prayer,
and when I do, I will trust Your answers.
—Amen

✿✿✿✿✿✿✿✿✿✿✿✿✿✿✿✿✿✿✿✿✿✿✿✿✿✿

When I've Made Mistakes

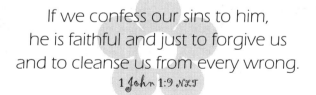

If we confess our sins to him,
he is faithful and just to forgive us
and to cleanse us from every wrong.

1 John 1:9 NLT

Mistakes: nobody
likes 'em but everybody makes 'em. And you're no different! When you commit the inevitable blunders of life (and you will), do your best to correct them, learn from them, and pray for the wisdom to avoid those same mistakes in the future. If you're successful, the missteps of today will become the stepping stones of tomorrow. And your life will become a non-stop learning experience.

Mistakes are the price you pay for being human; *repeated* mistakes are the price you pay for being stubborn. So don't be hardheaded: learn from your experiences—the first time!

Think About It

God is able to take mistakes,
when they are committed to Him,
and make of them something for
our good and for His glory.
Ruth Bell Graham

It is human to err;
it is devilish to remain willfully in error.
St. Augustine

Sometimes it happens that I can think of
nothing that needs confessing.
This is usually a sign that
I'm not paying attention.
Shirley Dobson

WHEN I'VE MADE MISTAKES

Q: When I make a mistake, why am I so afraid of what my friends will think?

A: Maybe it's because you're *too concerned* about what people think and *not concerned enough* about what God thinks. Instead of worrying about what "they" think (whoever "they" are), worry more about what "He" thinks (He, of course, being God). After all, whom should you *really* be trying to impress—"them" or Him?

A Prayer to the Father

✿✿✿✿✿✿✿✿✿✿✿✿✿✿✿✿✿✿✿✿✿✿✿✿✿✿✿✿✿✿✿✿

Lord, sometimes I make mistakes and fall short of your commandments. When I do, forgive me, Father. And help me learn from my mistakes so that I can be a better person *and* a better example to my friends and family. —Amen

✿✿✿✿✿✿✿✿✿✿✿✿✿✿✿✿✿✿✿✿✿✿✿✿✿✿✿✿✿✿✿✿

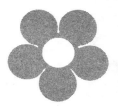

It's Life and It's Worth Celebrating

This is the day the LORD has made.
We will rejoice and be glad in it.
Psalm 118:24 *NLT*

What is the best day to celebrate life? This one!

Today and every day should be a time for celebration as we consider the Good News of God's free gift: salvation through Jesus Christ.

What do you expect from the day ahead? Are you expecting God to do wonderful things, or are you living beneath a cloud of worry and doubt?

The familiar words of Psalm 118:24 remind us of a profound yet simple truth: "This is the day which the LORD has made." Our duty, as believers, is to rejoice in God's marvelous creation. For Christians, every day begins and ends with God and His Son. Christ came to this earth to give us abundant life and eternal salvation. We give thanks to our Maker when we treasure each day. So with no further ado, let the celebration begin!

2 MINUTES A DAY

Think About It

The time for universal praise is sure
to come some day.
Let us begin to do our part now.
Hannah Whitall Smith

Preoccupy my thoughts with
your praise beginning today.
Joni Eareckson Tada

The best moment to praise God
is always the present one.
Marie T. Freeman

God is worthy of our praise
and is pleased when we come
before Him with thanksgiving.
Shirley Dobson

IT'S WORTH CELEBRATING

Q: If life is a celebration, why don't I feel like celebrating?

A: Perhaps all you need is an attitude adjustment: if so, start focusing more on the donut and less on the hole. But if you're feeling *really* sad or *deeply* depressed, TALK ABOUT IT with people who can help, starting with your parents. Then, don't hesitate to speak with your doctor, or your pastor, or your school counselor, or all of the above. Help is available. Ask for it. NOW!

A Prayer to the Father

Dear Lord, You have given me so many blessings, and as a way of saying "Thank You," I will celebrate. And, I will share my joy with my family, with my friends, and with my neighbors, this day and every day. —Amen

2 MINUTES A DAY

Too Much Stuff

No one can serve two masters.
The person will hate one master
and love the other, or will follow
one master and refuse to follow the other.
You cannot serve both God
and worldly riches.
Matthew 6:24 NCV

How much stuff is too much stuff?

Well, if your desire for stuff is getting in the way of your desire to know God, then you've got too much stuff—it's as simple as that.

Do you find yourself wrapped up in the concerns of the material world? If so, it's time to reorder your priorities by turning your thoughts and your prayers to more important matters. And, it's time to begin storing up riches that will endure throughout eternity: the spiritual kind.

Think About It

It's sobering to contemplate how much
time, effort, sacrifice, compromise,
and attention we give to acquiring
and increasing our supply of something
that is totally insignificant in eternity.
Anne Graham Lotz

Why is love of gold more potent
than love of souls?
Lottie Moon

Have you prayed about your resources
lately? Find out how God wants you
to use your time and your money.
No matter what it costs,
forsake all that is not of God.
Kay Arthur

TOO MUCH STUFF

A Timely Tip

✿✿✿✿✿✿✿✿✿✿✿✿✿✿✿✿✿✿✿✿✿✿✿✿✿✿✿✿✿✿✿✿✿✿✿

Generosity 101

Some of the best stuff you'll ever have is the stuff you give away.

✿✿✿✿✿✿✿✿✿✿✿✿✿✿✿✿✿✿✿✿✿✿✿✿✿✿✿✿✿✿✿✿✿✿✿

A Prayer to the Father

✿✿✿✿✿✿✿✿✿✿✿✿✿✿✿✿✿✿✿✿✿✿✿✿✿✿✿✿✿✿✿✿✿✿✿

Lord, my greatest possession is my relationship with You through Jesus Christ. You have promised that when I seek Your kingdom and Your righteousness, You will give me the things that I need. I will trust You completely, Lord, for my needs, both material and spiritual, this day and always. —Amen

✿✿✿✿✿✿✿✿✿✿✿✿✿✿✿✿✿✿✿✿✿✿✿✿✿✿✿✿✿✿✿✿✿✿✿

2 MINUTES A DAY

Pleasing People, Pleasing God

Obviously, I'm not trying to be
a people pleaser! No, I am trying
to please God. If I were still trying
to please people,
I would not be Christ's servant.

Galatians 1:10 *NLT*

If you're like most people, you seek the admiration of your friends, your classmates, and your family members. But the eagerness to please others should never overshadow your eagerness to please God. In every aspect of your life, pleasing your Heavenly Father should come first.

Would you like a time-tested formula for successful living? Here is a formula that is proven and true: Seek God's approval first and other people's approval later. Does this sound too simple? Perhaps it is simple, but it is also the only way to reap the marvelous riches that God has in store for you.

Think About It

It is comfortable to know that
we are responsible to God and
not to man. It is a small matter
to be judged of man's judgement.
Lottie Moon

Those who follow the crowd
usually get lost in it.
Rick Warren

You should forget about trying
to be popular with everybody
and start trying to be popular
with God Almighty.
Sam Jones

PLEASING PEOPLE, PLEASING GOD

And One More Thing . . .

↓   ↓   ↓

Make God's will the focus of your life day by day. If you seek to please Him and Him alone, you'll find yourself satisfied with life.

Kay Arthur

A Prayer to the Father

✿✿✿✿✿✿✿✿✿✿✿✿✿✿✿✿✿✿✿✿✿✿✿✿✿✿✿

Dear Lord, today I will worry less about pleasing other people and more about pleasing You. I will honor You with my thoughts, my actions, and my prayers. And I will worship You, Father, with thanksgiving in my heart, this day and forever. —Amen

✿✿✿✿✿✿✿✿✿✿✿✿✿✿✿✿✿✿✿✿✿✿✿✿✿✿✿

2 MINUTES A DAY

Taking God at His Word

As for God, his way is perfect.
All the Lord's promises prove true.
He is a shield for all who look
to him for protection.

Psalm 18:30 NLT

God has made quite a few promises to you, and He intends to keep every single one of them. You will find these promises in a book like no other: the Holy Bible. The Bible is your roadmap for life here on earth and for life eternal—as a believer, you are called upon to trust its promises, to follow its commandments, and to share its Good News.

God has made promises to all of humanity *and* to you. God's promises never fail and they never grow old. You must trust those promises and share them with your family, with your friends, and with the world . . . starting now . . . and ending never.

2 MINUTES A DAY

Think About It

Claim all of God's promises in the Bible.
Your sins, your worries, your life—
you may cast them all on Him.
Corrie ten Boom

Shake the dust from your past,
and move forward in His promises.
Kay Arthur

If we are not continually fed with
God's Word, we will starve spiritually.
Stormie Omartian

TAKING GOD AT HIS WORD

And One More Thing . . .

↓   ↓   ↓

God's Word is a light not only to
our path but to our thinking.
Place it in your heart today,
and you will never walk in darkness.
Joni Eareckson Tada

A Prayer to the Father

✿✿✿✿✿✿✿✿✿✿✿✿✿✿✿✿✿✿✿✿✿✿✿✿✿✿✿✿✿✿✿

Dear Lord, the Bible is Your gift to me. Let
me use it, let me trust it, and let me obey it,
today and every day that I live. —Amen

✿✿✿✿✿✿✿✿✿✿✿✿✿✿✿✿✿✿✿✿✿✿✿✿✿✿✿✿✿✿✿

Family
Matters

You must choose for yourselves today
whom you will serve . . . as for me
and my family, we will serve the Lord.
Joshua 24:15 NCV

Are you ever frustrated by your family? If so, welcome to the club. No family is perfect, and neither is yours. But, despite the occasional frustrations, disappointments, and hurt feelings of family life, your clan is God's gift to you. That little band of men, women, kids, and babies is a priceless treasure on temporary loan from the Father above. Give thanks to the Giver for the gift of family...and act accordingly.

Think About It

The family that prays together,
stays together.
Anonymous

A home is a place where we find direction.
Gigi Graham Tchividjian

There is so much compassion
and understanding that is gained
when we've experienced God's grace
firsthand within our own families.
Lisa Whelchel

FAMILY MATTERS

A Timely Tip

✿✿✿✿✿✿✿✿✿✿✿✿✿✿✿✿✿✿✿✿✿✿✿✿✿✿✿✿✿✿✿✿

Since you love them, tell them so! Let your family members know that you love them by the things you say and the things you do. And, never take your family for granted; they deserve your very best treatment!

✿✿✿✿✿✿✿✿✿✿✿✿✿✿✿✿✿✿✿✿✿✿✿✿✿✿✿✿✿✿✿✿

A Prayer to the Father

✿✿✿✿✿✿✿✿✿✿✿✿✿✿✿✿✿✿✿✿✿✿✿✿✿✿✿✿✿✿✿✿

Dear Lord, you have given me a wonderful gift: a loving family. Today and every day, let me show my family that I love them by the things that I say *and* the things that I do. —Amen

✿✿✿✿✿✿✿✿✿✿✿✿✿✿✿✿✿✿✿✿✿✿✿✿✿✿✿✿✿✿✿✿

Attitude Adjustments

And now, dear brothers and sisters,
let me say one more thing as I close
this letter. Fix your thoughts on what
is true and honorable and right.
Think about things that are pure
and lovely and admirable. Think
about things that are excellent
and worthy of praise.

Philippians 4:8 NLT

What's your attitude

today? Are you fearful, angry, bored, or worried? Are you worried more about pleasing your friends than about pleasing your God? Are you confused, bitter or pessimistic? If so, God wants to have a little talk with you.

God created you in His own image, and He wants you to experience joy and abundance. But, God will not force His joy upon you; you must claim it for yourself. So today, and every day hereafter, celebrate this life that God has given you. Think optimistically about yourself and your future. Give thanks to the One who has given you everything, and trust in your heart that He wants to give you so much more.

Think About It

I could go through this day oblivious
to the miracles all around me,
or I could tune in and "enjoy."
Gloria Gaither

The things we think are the things that
feed our souls. If we think on pure
and lovely things, we shall grow pure
and lovely like them;
and the converse is equally true.
Hannah Whitall Smith

The Reference Point for the Christian is
the Bible. All values, judgments,
and attitudes must be gauged
in relationship to this Reference Point.
Ruth Bell Graham

ATTITUDE ADJUSTMENTS

A Timely Tip

✿✿✿✿✿✿✿✿✿✿✿✿✿✿✿✿✿✿✿✿✿✿✿✿✿✿✿✿✿✿✿✿

Maybe it's just your attitude *but . . .* If you have persistent feelings of sadness or despair—or if you know somebody who does—seek help immediately. It might be depression, a condition that's both serious and treatable. So don't delay.

✿✿✿✿✿✿✿✿✿✿✿✿✿✿✿✿✿✿✿✿✿✿✿✿✿✿✿✿✿✿✿✿

A Prayer to the Father

✿✿✿✿✿✿✿✿✿✿✿✿✿✿✿✿✿✿✿✿✿✿✿✿✿✿✿✿✿✿✿✿

Lord, I pray for an attitude that is Christlike. Whatever my situation, whether good or bad, happy or sad, let me respond with an attitude of optimism, faith, and love for You. —Amen

✿✿✿✿✿✿✿✿✿✿✿✿✿✿✿✿✿✿✿✿✿✿✿✿✿✿✿✿✿✿✿✿

Spiritual Growing Pains

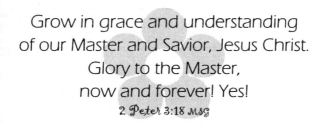

Grow in grace and understanding
of our Master and Savior, Jesus Christ.
Glory to the Master,
now and forever! Yes!

2 Peter 3:18 MSG

Are you a fully-grown girl?

Physically: maybe so. But spiritually? No way! And thank goodness that you're not! Even if you're a very mature person—even if you're a righteous, spiritual, godly woman—you've still got lots of room to grow.

The 19th-century writer Hannah Whitall Smith observed, "The maturity of a Christian experience cannot be reached in a moment." No kidding. In truth, the search for spiritual growth lasts a lifetime.

When we cease to grow, either emotionally or spiritually, we do ourselves and our families a profound disservice. But, if we study God's Word, if we obey His commandments, and if we live in the center of His will, we will not be "stagnant" believers; we will, instead, be growing Christians . . . and that's exactly what God wants for our lives. Come to think of it, that's exactly what *you* should want, too.

2 MINUTES A DAY

Think About It

You are either becoming more like
Christ every day or you're
becoming less like Him.
There is no neutral position in the Lord.
Stormie Omartian

Walking in faith brings you to
the Word of God. There you will be
healed, cleansed, fed, nurtured,
equipped, and matured.
Kay Arthur

Keep your face upturned to Christ
as the flowers do to the sun.
Look, and your soul shall live and grow.
Hannah Whitall Smith

SPIRITUAL GROWING PAINS

And One More Thing . . .

↓ ↓ ↓

I'm not what I want to be.
I'm not what I'm going to be.
But, thank God, I'm not what I was!
Gloria Gaither

A Prayer to the Father

✿✿✿✿✿✿✿✿✿✿✿✿✿✿✿✿✿✿✿✿✿✿✿✿✿✿✿✿✿✿✿✿✿✿✿✿✿

Dear Lord, when I open my heart to You,
I am blessed. Today, I will accept Your love
and Your wisdom. And, I will do my best to
continue to grow in my faith every day that
I live. —Amen

✿✿✿✿✿✿✿✿✿✿✿✿✿✿✿✿✿✿✿✿✿✿✿✿✿✿✿✿✿✿✿✿✿✿✿✿✿

For God So Loved the World

For God loved the world in this way:
He gave His only Son, so that everyone
who believes in Him will not perish
but have eternal life.

John 3:16 HCSB

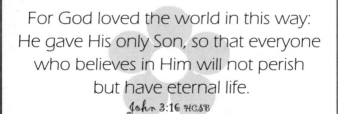

How much does God love you? As long as you're alive, you'll never be able to figure it out because God's love is just too big to comprehend. But this much we know: God loves you so much that He sent His Son, Jesus to come to this earth and to die for you! And, when you accepted Jesus into your heart, God gave you a gift that is more precious than gold: the gift of eternal life.

God's love is bigger and more powerful than anybody can imagine, but His love is *very* real. So do yourself a favor right now: accept God's love with open arms and welcome His Son, Jesus into your heart. When you do, your life will be changed today, tomorrow, and forever.

Think About It

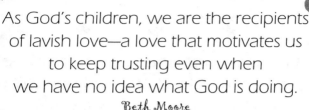

As God's children, we are the recipients
of lavish love—a love that motivates us
to keep trusting even when
we have no idea what God is doing.
Beth Moore

There is no pit so deep
that God's love is not deeper still.
Corrie ten Boom

Believing that you are loved
will set you free to be who
God created you to be.
So rest in His love and just be yourself.
Lisa Whelchel

FOR GOD SO LOVED THE WORLD

And One More Thing . . .

↓   ↓   ↓

We must mirror God's love in the midst
of a troubled world. We are the mirrors
of God's love, so we may show
Jesus by our lives.

Corrie ten Boom

A Prayer to the Father

✿✿✿✿✿✿✿✿✿✿✿✿✿✿✿✿✿✿✿✿✿✿✿✿✿✿✿✿✿✿✿✿✿✿✿

Dear Lord, thank You for loving me. And
thank You for sending Your Son Jesus to
this earth so that I can receive Your gift o
eternal love and eternal life. I will praise You
Dear God, today, tomorrow, and forever
—Amen

✿✿✿✿✿✿✿✿✿✿✿✿✿✿✿✿✿✿✿✿✿✿✿✿✿✿✿✿✿✿✿✿✿✿✿

More Good Stuff

Quotations and Bible Verses by Topic

Hope

Without wavering, let us hold tightly
to the hope we say we have,
for God can be trusted
to keep his promise.
Hebrews 10:23 NLT

The most profane word we use is
"hopeless." When you say a situation
or person is hopeless, you are slamming
the door in the face of God.
Kathy Troccoli

Hope is nothing more than
the expectation of those things
which faith has believed to
be truly promised by God.
John Calvin

Generosity

If you have two coats, give one to
the poor. If you have food, share it
with those who are hungry.

Luke 3:11 NLT

The measure of a life, after all,
is not its duration but its donation.

Corrie ten Boom

Nothing is really ours until we share it.

C. S. Lewis

All kindness and good deeds,
we must keep silent. The result will be
an inner reservoir of power.

Catherine Marshall

MORE GOOD STUFF

Kindness

Be kind to each other, tenderhearted,
forgiving one another, just as God
through Christ has forgiven you.
Ephesians 4:32 NLT

Kindness in this world will do much
to help others, not only to come into
the light, but also to grow in grace
day by day.
Fanny Crosby

The nicest thing we can do for
our heavenly Father is to be kind
to one of His children.
St. Teresa of Avila

Love

See to it that you really do
love each other intensely
with all your hearts.
1 Peter 1:22 NLT

Life is immortal, love eternal;
death is nothing but a horizon,
and a horizon is only the limit of our vision.
Corrie ten Boom

Love is not grabbing, or self-centered,
or selfish. Real love is being able
to contribute to the happiness
of another person without expecting
to get anything in return.
James Dobson

MORE GOOD STUFF

Attitude

And now, dear brothers and sisters,
let me say one more thing as I close this
letter. Fix your thoughts on what is true
and honorable and right. Think about
things that are pure and lovely and
admirable. Think about things that are
excellent and worthy of praise.

Philippians 4:8 NLT

No more imperfect thoughts.
No more sad memories. No more
ignorance. My redeemed body will have
a redeemed mind. Grant me a foretaste of
that perfect mind as you mirror
your thoughts in me today.

Joni Eareckson Tada

Forgiveness

Sometimes, we need a housecleaning
of the heart.
Catherine Marshall

How often should you forgive
the other person? Only as many times
as you want God to forgive you!
Marie T. Freeman

Love is an attribute of God.
To love others is evidence of
a genuine faith.
Kay Arthur

After the forgiving comes laughter,
a deeper love—and further
opportunities to forgive.
Ruth Bell Graham

MORE GOOD STUFF

Tough Times

We also have joy with our troubles,
because we know that these troubles
produce patience. And patience produces
character, and character produces hope.

Romans 5:3, 4 NCV

Often God shuts a door in our face
so that he can open the door through
which he wants us to go.

Catherine Marshall

If all struggles and sufferings were
eliminated, the spirit would no more
reach maturity than would the child.

Elisabeth Elliot

2 MINUTES A DAY

Faith

The fundamental fact of existence is
that this trust in God, this faith,
is the firm foundation under everything
that makes life worth living.
Hebrews 11:1 MSG

When you and I place our faith in
Jesus Christ and invite Him to come live
within us, the Holy Spirit comes upon us,
and the power of God overshadows us,
and the life of Jesus is born within us.
Anne Graham Lotz

Faith in faith is pointless. Faith in a living,
active God moves mountains.
Beth Moore

MORE GOOD STUFF

Self-acceptance

Blessed are those who
do not condemn themselves.
Romans 14:22 NLT

You cannot belong to anyone else
until you belong to yourself.
Pearl Bailey

Find satisfaction in him who made you,
and only then find satisfaction in
yourself as part of his creation.
St. Augustine

A healthy self-identity is seeing yourself
as God sees you—no more and no less.
Josh McDowell

2 MINUTES A DAY

Dreams

You are my hope, O Lord God;
You are my trust from my youth.
Psalm 71:5 NKJV

Always stay connected to people
and seek out things that bring you joy.
Dream with abandon. Pray confidently.
Barbara Johnson

You pay God a compliment by
asking great things of Him.
St. Teresa of Avila

You cannot out-dream God.
John Eldredge

MORE GOOD STUFF

Thanksgiving

I will thank you, Lord, with all my heart;
I will tell of all the marvelous things you
have done. I will be filled with joy
because of you. I will sing praises
to your name, O Most High.

Psalm 9:1, 2 NLT

The act of thanksgiving is a demonstration
of the fact that you are going to trust
and believe God.

Kay Arthur

The best way to show my gratitude
to God is to accept everything,
even my problems, with joy.

Mother Teresa

2 MINUTES A DAY

Accepting the Past

The Lord says, "Forget what happened
before, and do not think about
the past. Look at the new thing I am
going to do. It is already happening."
Isaiah 43:18, 19 NCV

We can't just put our pasts behind us.
We've got to put our pasts in front of God.
Beth Moore

If you are God's child, you are no longer
bound to your past or to what you were.
You are a brand new creature
in Christ Jesus.
Kay Arthur

God forgets the past. Imitate him.
Max Lucado

MORE GOOD STUFF

Lifetime Learning

If you listen to constructive criticism,
you will be at home among the wise.
Proverbs 15:31 *NLT*

Grow, dear friends, but grow,
I beseech you, in God's way,
which is the only true way.
Hannah Whitall Smith

The process of living seems to consist in
coming to realize truths so ancient and
simple that, if stated, they sound
like barren platitudes. They cannot sound
otherwise to those who have not had
the relevant experience: that is why there
is no real teaching of such truths possible
and every generation starts from scratch.
C. S. Lewis

2 MINUTES A DAY

Purpose

We know that all things work together for
the good of those who love God: those
who are called according to His purpose.
Romans 8:28 HCSB

We are most vulnerable to the piercing
winds of doubt when we distance
ourselves from the mission and fellowship
to which Christ has called us.
Joni Eareckson Tada

When we have the Spirit of God, He gives
the insight to understand what God is
doing or desires to do in and through us.
Franklin Graham

God is more concerned with the direction
of your life than with its speed.
Marie T. Freeman

MORE GOOD STUFF

Materialism

For where your treasure is,
there your heart will be also.
Luke 12:34 NKJV

If you want to be truly happy, you won't
find it on an endless quest for more stuff.
You'll find it in receiving God's generosity
and then passing that generosity along.
Bill Hybels

It's sobering to contemplate how much
time, effort, sacrifice, compromise,
and attention we give to acquiring
and increasing our supply of something
that is totally insignificant in eternity.
Anne Graham Lotz

God's Love

For the Lord is good. His unfailing love
continues forever, and his faithfulness
continues to each generation.
Psalm 100:5 NLT

When once we are assured that
God is good, then there can be
nothing left to fear.
Hannah Whitall Smith

The great love of God is an ocean
without a bottom or a shore.
C. H. Spurgeon

God is a God of unconditional,
unremitting love, a love that corrects
and chastens but never ceases.
Kay Arthur

MORE GOOD STUFF

God's Protection

The Lord keeps watch over you as
you come and go, both now and forever.
Psalm 121:8 NLT

A mighty fortress is our God.
Martin Luther

God walks with us. He scoops us up
in His arms or simply sits with us in silent
strength until we cannot avoid
the awesome recognition that yes,
even now, He is here.
Gloria Gaither

God is always sufficient in
perfect proportion to our need.
Beth Moore

2 MINUTES A DAY

Salvation

The crucial question for each of us is this:
What do you think of Jesus,
and do you yet have a personal
acquaintance with Him?
Hannah Whitall Smith

Salvation involves so much more than
knowing facts about Jesus Christ, or
even having special feelings toward
Jesus Christ. Salvation comes to us when,
by an act of will, we receive Christ
as our Savior and Lord.
Warren Wiersbe

I now know the power of the risen Lord!
He lives! The dawn of Easter has broken
in my own soul! My night is gone!
Mrs. Charles E. Cowman

MORE GOOD STUFF

I assure you,
anyone who
believes in me
already has
eternal life.

John 6:47 NLT